Theodore Roosevelt

True Americanism

Being Four Essays
Selected from the Collection Entitled
"American Ideals"

By

Theodore Roosevelt

Patrick Henry University Press
Colorado Springs, Colorado

True Americanism

by
Theodore Roosevelt

ISBN: 1-58963-979-0

Reprinted from the 1897 edition

Patrick Henry University Press
An Imprint of Fredonia Books
Colorado Springs, Colorado
http://www.patrickhenryuniversitypress.com

In order to make original editions of historical works available to scholars at an economical price, this facsimile of the original edition of 1897 is reproduced from the best available copy and has been digitally enhanced to improve legibility, but the text remains unaltered to retain historical authenticity.

PREFACE.

IT is not difficult to be virtuous in a cloistered and negative way. Neither is it difficult to succeed, after a fashion, in active life, if one is content to disregard the considerations which bind honorable and upright men. But it is by no means easy to combine honesty and efficiency; and yet it is absolutely necessary, in order to do any work really worth doing. It is not hard, while sitting in one's study, to devise admirable plans for the betterment of politics and of social conditions; but in practice it too often proves very hard to make any such plan work at all, no matter how imperfectly. Yet the effort must continually be made, under penalty of

constant retrogression in our political
life.

No one quality or one virtue is enough
to insure success ; vigor, honesty, common sense,—all are needed. The practical man is merely rendered more
noxious by his practical ability if he
employs it wrongly, whether from igno-
rance or from lack of morality; while the
doctrinaire, the man of theories, whether
written or spoken, is useless if he cannot
also act.

These essays are written on behalf of
the many men who do take an actual
part in trying practically to bring about
the conditions for which we somewhat
vaguely hope ; on behalf of the under-
officers in that army which, with much
stumbling, halting, and slipping, many
mistakes and shortcomings, and many
painful failures, does, nevertheless,
through weary strife, accomplish something toward raising the standard of
public life.

Preface

We feel that the doer is better than the critic and that the man who strives stands far above the man who stands aloof, whether he thus stands aloof because of pessimism or because of sheer weakness. To borrow a simile from the football field, we believe that men must play fair, but that there must be no shirking, and that success can only come to the player who " hits the line hard."

THEODORE ROOSEVELT.

SAGAMORE HILL,
October, 1897.

CONTENTS

CONTENTS

AMERICAN IDEALS

AMERICAN IDEALS

IN his noteworthy book on *National Life and Character*, Mr. Pearson says: "The countrymen of Chatham and Wellington, of Washington and Lincoln, in short the citizens of every historic state, are richer by great deeds that have formed the national character, by winged words that have passed into current speech, by the examples of lives and labors consecrated to the service of the commonwealth." In other words, every great nation owes to the men whose lives have formed part of its greatness not merely the material effect of what they did, not merely the laws they placed upon the statute books or the victories they won over armed foes, but also the

immense but indefinable moral influence
produced by their deeds and words themselves upon the national character. It
would be difficult to exaggerate the material effects of the careers of Washington
and of Lincoln upon the United States.
Without Washington we should probably
never have won our independence of the
British Crown, and we should almost
certainly have failed to become a great
nation, remaining instead a cluster of
jangling little communities, drifting
toward the type of government prevalent
in Spanish America. Without Lincoln
we might perhaps have failed to keep the
political unity we had won; and even if,
as is possible, we had kept it, both the
struggle by which it was kept and the
results of this struggle would have been
so different that the effect upon our national history could not have failed to be
profound. Yet the nation's debt to these
men is not confined to what it owes them
for its material well-being, incalculable

though this debt is. Beyond the fact
that we are an independent and united
people, with half a continent as our
heritage, lies the fact that every American is richer by the heritage of the noble
deeds and noble words of Washington
and of Lincoln. Each of us who reads
the Gettysburg speech or the second in-
augural address of the greatest American of the nineteenth century, or who
studies the long campaigns and lofty
statesmanship of that other American
who was even greater, cannot but feel
within him that lift toward things higher
and nobler which can never be bestowed
by the enjoyment of mere material prosperity.

It is not only the country which these
men helped to make and helped to save
that is ours by inheritance; we inherit
also all that is best and highest in their
characters and in their lives. We inherit
from Lincoln and from the might of Lincoln's generation not merely the freedom

of those who once were slaves; for we inherit also the fact of the freeing of them, we inherit the glory and the honor and the wonder of the deed that was done, no less than the actual results of the deed when done. The bells that rang at the passage of the Emancipation Proclamation still ring in Whittier's ode; and as men think over the real nature of the triumph then scored for humankind their hearts shall ever throb as they cannot over the greatest industrial success or over any victory won at a less cost than ours.

The captains and the armies who, after long years of dreary campaigning and bloody, stubborn fighting, brought to a close the Civil War have likewise left us even more than a reunited realm. The material effect of what they did is shown in the fact that the same flag flies from the Great Lakes to the Rio Grande, and all the people of the United States are richer because they are one people and

6

not many, because they belong to one
great nation and not to a contemptible
knot of struggling nationalities. But
besides this, besides the material results
of the Civil War, we are all, North and
South, incalculably richer for its memo-
ries. We are the richer for each grim
campaign, for each hard-fought battle.
We are the richer for valor displayed
alike by those who fought so valiantly
for the right, and by those who, no less
valiantly, fought for what they deemed
the right. We have in us nobler capaci-
ties for what is great and good because
of the infinite woe and suffering and
because of the splendid ultimate triumph.

In the same way that we are the better
for the deeds of our mighty men who
have served the nation well, so we are
the worse for the deeds and the words of
those who have striven to bring evil on
the land. Most fortunately we have
been free from the peril of the most dangerous of all examples. We have not

had to fight the influence exerted over the minds of eager and ambitious men by the career of the military adventurer who heads some successful revolutionary or separatist movement. No man works such incalculable woe to a free country as he who teaches young men that one of the paths to glory, renown, and temporal success lies along the line of armed resistance to the Government, of its attempted overthrow.

Yet if we are free from the peril of this example, there are other perils from which we are not free. All through our career we have had to war against a tendency to regard, in the individual and the nation alike, as most important, things that are of comparatively little importance. We rightfully value success, but sometimes we overvalue it, for we tend to forget that success may be obtained by means which should make it abhorred and despised by every honorable man. One section of the community deifies as

" smartness " the kind of trickery which enables a man without conscience to succeed in the financial or political world. Another section of the community deifies violent homicidal lawlessness. If ever our people as a whole adopt these views, then we shall have proved that we are unworthy of the heritage our forefathers left us ; and our country will go down in ruin.

The people that do harm in the end are not the wrong-doers whom all execrate ; they are the men who do not do quite as much wrong, but who are applauded instead of being execrated. The career of Benedict Arnold has done us no harm as a nation because of the universal horror it inspired. The men who have done us harm are those who have advocated disunion, but have done it so that they have been enabled to keep their political position; who have advocated repudiation of debts, or other financial dishonesty, but have kept their standing

9

in the community; who preach the doctrines of anarchy, but refrain from action that will bring them within the pale of the law; for these men lead thousands astray by the fact that they go unpunished or even rewarded for their misdeeds.

It is unhappily true that we inherit the evil as well as the good done by those who have gone before us, and in the one case as in the other the influence extends far beyond the mere material effects. The foes of order harm quite as much by example as by what they actually accomplish. So it is with the equally dangerous criminals of the wealthy classes. The conscienceless stock speculator who acquires wealth by swindling his fellows, by debauching judges and corrupting legislatures, and who ends his days with the reputation of being among the richest men in America, exerts over the minds of the rising generation an influence worse than that of the average murderer or bandit, because his career is even more

dazzling in its success and even more
dangerous in its effects upon the community. Any one who reads the essays
of Charles Francis Adams and Henry
Adams, entitled "A Chapter of Erie,"
and "The Gold Conspiracy in New
York," will read about the doings of
men whose influence for evil upon the
community is more potent than that of
any band of anarchists or train robbers.

There are other members of our mer-
cantile community who, being perfectly
honest themselves, nevertheless do almost as much damage as the dishonest.
The professional labor agitator, with all
his reckless incendiarism of speech, can
do no more harm than the narrow, hard,
selfish merchant or manufacturer who de-
liberately sets himself to keep the laborers
he employs in a condition of dependence
which will render them helpless to combine against him; and every such merchant or manufacturer who rises to
sufficient eminence leaves the record of

his name and deeds as a legacy of evil to all who come after him.

But of course the worst foes of America are the foes to that orderly liberty without which our Republic must speedily perish. The reckless labor agitator who arouses the mob to riot and bloodshed is in the last analysis the most dangerous of the workingman's enemies. This man is a real peril; and so is his sympathizer, the legislator, who to catch votes denounces the judiciary and the military because they put down mobs. We Americans have, on the whole, a right to be optimists; but it is mere folly to blind ourselves to the fact that there are some black clouds on the horizon of our future.

During the summer of 1894, every American capable of thinking must at times have pondered very gravely over certain features of the national character which were brought into unpleasant prominence by the course of events. The demagogue, in all his forms, is as characteristic an

evil of a free society as the courtier is of
a despotism; and the attitude of many
of our public men at the time of the great
strike in July, 1894, was such as to call
down on their heads the hearty condemnation of every American who wishes
well to his country.   It would be difficult
to overestimate the damage done by the
example and action of a man like Governor Altgeld of Illinois.   Whether he is
honest or not in his beliefs is not of the
slightest consequence. He is as emphatically the foe of decent government
as Tweed himself, and is capable of doing
far more damage than Tweed.   The Governor, who began his career by pardoning
anarchists, and whose most noteworthy
feat since was his bitter and undignified,
but fortunately futile, campaign against
the election of the upright judge who
sentenced the anarchists, is the foe of
every true American and is the foe particularly of every honest workingman.
With such a man it was to be expected

that he should in time of civic commotion
act as the foe of the law-abiding and the
friend of the lawless classes, and endeavor,
in company with the lowest and most
abandoned office-seeking politicians, to
prevent proper measures being taken to
prevent riot and to punish the rioters.
Had it not been for the admirable action
of the Federal Government, Chicago
would have seen a repetition of what oc-
curred during the Paris Commune, while
Illinois would have been torn by a fierce
social war; and for all the horrible waste
of life that this would have entailed Governor Altgeld would have been primarily
responsible. It was a most fortunate
thing that the action at Washington was
so quick and so emphatic. Senator Davis
of Minnesota set the key of patriotism at
the time when men were still puzzled and
hesitated. The President and Attorney-
General Olney acted with equal wisdom
and courage, and the danger was averted.
The completeness of the victory of the

Federal authorities, representing the cause of law and order, has been perhaps one reason why it was so soon forgotten; and now not a few short-sighted people need to be reminded that when we were on the brink of an almost terrific explosion the governor of Illinois did his best to work to this country a measure of harm as great as any ever planned by Benedict Arnold, and that we were saved by the resolute action of the Federal judiciary and of the regular army. Moreover, Governor Altgeld, though pre-eminent, did not stand alone on his unenviable prominence. Governor Waite of Colorado stood with him. Most of the Populist governors of the Western States, and the Republican governor of California and the Democratic governor of North Dakota shared the shame with him; and it makes no difference whether in catering to riotous mobs they paid heed to their own timidity and weakness, or to that spirit of blatant demagogism which, more than any other, jeopardizes the existence of free institutions. On the other hand, the action of the then Governor of Ohio, Mr. McKinley, entitled him to the gratitude of all good citizens.

Every true American, every man who thinks, and who if the occasion comes is ready to act, may do well to ponder upon the evil wrought by the lawlessness of the disorderly classes when once they are able to elect their own chiefs to power. If the Government generally got into the hands of men such as Altgeld, the Republic would go to pieces in a year; and it would be right that it should go to pieces, for the election of such men shows that the people electing them are unfit to be entrusted with self-government.

There are, however, plenty of wrong-doers besides those who commit the overt act. Too much cannot be said against the men of wealth who sacrifice everything to getting wealth. There is not in the world a more ignoble character than

the mere money-getting American, in-
sensible to every duty, regardless of every
principle, bent only on amassing a fortune, and putting his fortune only to the
basest uses — whether these uses be to
speculate in stocks and wreck railroads
himself, or to allow his son to lead a life
of foolish and expensive idleness and
gross debauchery, or to purchase some
scoundrel of high social position, foreign
or native, for his daughter.   Such a man
is only the more dangerous if he occasionally does some deed like founding a
college or endowing a church, which
makes those good people who are also
foolish forget his real iniquity.   These
men are equally careless of the working-
men, whom they oppress, and of the
State, whose existence they imperil.
There are not very many of them, but
there is a very great number of men who
approach more or less closely to the type,
and, just in so far as they do so approach,
they are curses to the country. The man

who is content to let politics go from bad
to worse, jesting at the corruption of
politicians, the man who is content to
see the maladministration of justice without an immediate and resolute effort to
reform it, is shirking his duty and is pre-
paring the way for infinite woe in the
future. Hard, brutal indifference to the
right, and an equally brutal short-sight-
edness as to the inevitable results of corruption and injustice are baleful beyond
measure; and yet they are characteristic
of a great many Americans who think
themselves perfectly respectable, and
who are considered thriving, prosperous
men by their easy-going fellow-citizens.

Another class, merging into this, and
only less dangerous, is that of the men
whose ideals are purely material. These
are the men who are willing to go for
good government when they think it will
pay, but who measure everything by the
shop-till; the people who are unable to
appreciate any quality that is not a mer-

cantile commodity; who do not understand that a poet may do far more for a
country than the owner of a nail factory;
who do not realize that no amount of
commercial prosperity can supply the
lack of the heroic virtues, or can in itself
solve the terrible social problems which
all the civilized world is now facing.
The mere materialist is, above all things,
short-sighted. In a recent article, Mr.
Edward Atkinson casually mentioned
that the regular army could now render
the country no "effective or useful service." Two months before this sapient
remark was printed the regular army
had saved Chicago from the fate of Paris
in 1870 and had prevented a terrible
social war in the West. At the end of
this article Mr. Atkinson indulged in a
curious rhapsody against the navy, de-
nouncing its existence and being especially wrought up, not because war-ves-
sels take life, but because they "destroy
commerce." To men of a certain kind,

trade and property are far more sacred than life or honor, of far more consequence than the great thoughts and lofty emotions which alone make a nation mighty. They believe, with a faith almost touching in its utter feebleness, that "the Angel of Peace, draped in a garment of untaxed calico," has given her final message to men when she has implored them to devote all their energies to producing oleomargarine at a quarter of a cent less a firkin, or to importing woollens for a fraction less than they can be made at home. These solemn prattlers strive after an ideal in which they shall happily unite the imagination of a green-grocer with the heart of a Bengalee baboo. They are utterly incapable of feeling one thrill of generous emotion, or the slightest throb of that pulse which gives to the world statesmen, patriots, warriors, and poets, and which makes a nation other than a cumberer of the world's surface. In the concluding page

of his article Mr. Atkinson, complacently
advancing his panacea, his quack cure-
all, says that "all evil powers of the
world will go down before" a policy of
"reciprocity of trade without obstruc-
tion"! Fatuity can go no farther.

No Populist who wishes a currency
based on corn and cotton stands in more
urgent need of applied common sense
than does the man who believes that the
adoption of any policy, no matter what,
in reference to our foreign commerce will
cut that tangled knot of social well-being
and misery at which the fingers of the
London free-trader clutch as helplessly as
those of the Berlin protectionist. Such a
man represents individually an almost
imponderable element in the work and
thought of the community; but in the
aggregate he stands for a real danger, because he stands for a feeling evident of late
years among many respectable people.
The people who pride themselves upon
having a purely commercial ideal are

apparently unaware that such an ideal is as essentially mean and sordid as any in the world; and that no bandit community of the Middle Ages can have led a more unlovely life than would be the life of men to whom trade and manufactures were everything, and to whom such words as national honor and glory, as courage and daring, and loyalty and unselfishness had become meaningless. The merely material, the merely commercial ideal, the ideal of the men "whose fatherland is the till," is in its very essence debasing and lowering. It is as true now as ever it was that no man and no nation shall live by bread alone. Thrift and industry are indispensable virtues; but they are not all-sufficient. We must base our appeals for civic and national betterment on nobler grounds than those of mere business expediency.

We have examples enough and to spare that tend to evil; nevertheless, for our good fortune, the men who have most

impressed themselves upon the thought
of the nation have left behind them
careers the influence of which must tell
for good. The unscrupulous speculator
who rises to enormous wealth by swindling his neighbor; the capitalist who op-
presses the workingman; the agitator
who wrongs the workingman yet more
deeply by trying to teach him to rely not
upon himself, but partly upon the charity
of individuals or of the State and partly
upon mob violence; the man in public life
who is a demagogue or corrupt, and the
newspaper writer who fails to attack him
because of his corruption, or who slan-
derously assails him when he is honest;
the political leader who, cursed by some
obliquity of moral or of mental vision,
seeks to produce sectional or social strife
—all these, though important in their
day, have hitherto failed to leave any
lasting impress upon the life of the
nation. The men who have profoundly
influenced the growth of our national

character have been in most cases precisely those men whose influence was for the best and was strongly felt as antagonistic to the worst tendency of the age. The great writers who have written in prose or verse have done much for us. The great orators whose burning words on behalf of liberty, of union, of honest government, have rung through our legislative halls have done even more. Most of all has been done by the men who have spoken to us through deeds and not words, or whose words have gathered their especial charm and significance because they came from men who did speak in deeds. A nation's greatness lies in its possibility of achievement in the present, and nothing helps it more than the consciousness of achievement in the past.

TRUE AMERICANISM

TRUE AMERICANISM

PATRIOTISM was once defined as "the last refuge of a scoundrel"; and somebody has recently remarked that when Dr. Johnson gave this definition he was ignorant of the infinite possibilities contained in the word "reform." Of course both gibes were quite justifiable, in so far as they were aimed at people who use noble names to cloak base purposes. Equally, of course, the man shows little wisdom and a low sense of duty who fails to see that love of country is one of the elemental virtues, even though scoundrels play upon it for their own selfish ends; and, inasmuch as abuses continually grow up in civic life

as in all other kinds of life, the statesman
is indeed a weakling who hesitates to
reform these abuses because the word
"reform" is often on the lips of men
who are silly or dishonest.

What is true of patriotism and reform
is true also of Americanism. There are
plenty of scoundrels always ready to try
to belittle reform movements or to bolster
up existing iniquities in the name of
Americanism; but this does not alter
the fact that the man who can do most
in this country is and must be the man
whose Americanism is most sincere and
intense. Outrageous though it is to use
a noble idea as a cloak for evil, it is still
worse to assail the noble idea itself because it can thus be used. The men who
do iniquity in the name of patriotism, of
reform, of Americanism, are merely one
small division of the class that has always
existed and will always exist,— the class
of hypocrites and demagogues, the class
that is always prompt to steal the watch-

words of righteousness and use them in the interests of evil-doing.

The stoutest and truest Americans are the very men who have the least sympathy with the people who invoke the spirit of Americanism to aid what is vicious in our government or to throw obstacles in the way of those who strive to reform it. It is contemptible to oppose a movement for good because that movement has already succeeded somewhere else, or to champion an existing abuse because our people have always been wedded to it. To appeal to national prejudice against a given reform movement is in every way unworthy and silly. It is as childish to denounce free trade because England has adopted it as to advocate it for the same reason. It is eminently proper, in dealing with the tariff, to consider the effect of tariff legislation in time past upon other nations as well as the effect upon our own; but in drawing conclusions it is in the last degree foolish to try to excite prejudice against one system because it is in vogue in some given country, or to try to excite prejudice in its favor because the economists of that country have found that it was suited to their own peculiar needs. In attempting to solve our difficult problem of municipal government it is mere folly to refuse to profit by whatever is good in the examples of Manchester and Berlin because these cities are foreign, exactly as it is mere folly blindly to copy their examples without reference to our own totally different conditions. As for the absurdity of declaiming against civil-service reform, for instance, as "Chinese," because written examinations have been used in China, it would be quite as wise to declaim against gunpowder because it was first utilized by the same people. In short, the man who, whether from mere dull fatuity or from an active interest in misgovernment, tries to appeal to American prejudice against things foreign, so as to induce Americans to oppose any measure for good, should be looked on by his fellow-countrymen with the heartiest contempt. So much for the men who appeal to the spirit of Americanism to sustain us in wrong-doing. But we must never let our contempt for these men blind us to the nobility of the idea which they strive to degrade.

We Americans have many grave problems to solve, many threatening evils to fight, and many deeds to do, if, as we hope and believe, we have the wisdom, the strength, the courage, and the virtue to do them. But we must face facts as they are. We must neither surrender ourselves to a foolish optimism, nor succumb to a timid and ignoble pessimism. Our nation is that one among all the nations of the earth which holds in its hands the fate of the coming years. We enjoy exceptional advantages, and are menaced by exceptional dangers; and all signs indicate that we shall either fail greatly or

31

succeed greatly. I firmly believe that we
shall succeed; but we must not foolishly
blink the dangers by which we are threat-
ened, for that is the way to fail. On the
contrary, we must soberly set to work to
find out all we can about the existence
and extent of every evil, must acknow-
ledge it to be such, and must then attack
it with unyielding resolution. There are
many such evils, and each must be fought
after a separate fashion; yet there is one
quality which we must bring to the solu-
tion of every problem,—that is, an intense
and fervid Americanism. We shall never
be successful over the dangers that con-
front us; we shall never achieve true
greatness, nor reach the lofty ideal which
thé founders and preservers of our mighty
Federal Republic have set before us, unless we are Americans in heart and soul,
in spirit and purpose, keenly alive to the
responsibility implied in the very name
of American, and proud beyond measure
of the glorious privilege of bearing it.

There are two or three sides to the question of Americanism, and two or three senses in which the word "Americanism" can be used to express the antithesis of what is unwholesome and undesirable. In the first place we wish to be broadly American and national, as opposed to being local or sectional. We do not wish, in politics, in literature, or in art, to develop that unwholesome parochial spirit, that over-exaltation of the little community at the expense of the great nation, which produces what has been described as the patriotism of the village, the patriotism of the belfry. Politically, the indulgence of this spirit was the chief cause of the calamities which befell the ancient republics of Greece, the mediæval republics of Italy, and the petty States of Germany as it was in the 18th century. It is this spirit of provincial patriotism, this inability to take a view of broad adhesion to the whole nation, that has been the chief among the causes

3

that have produced such anarchy in the
South American States, and which have
resulted in presenting to us, not one great
Spanish-American federal nation stretching from the Rio Grande to Cape Horn,
but a squabbling multitude of revolution-
ridden States, not one of which stands
even in the second rank as a power.
However, politically this question of
American nationality has been settled
once for all. We are no longer in danger
of repeating in our history the shameful
and contemptible disasters that have be-
fallen the Spanish possessions on this
continent since they threw off the yoke
of Spain. Indeed there is, all through our
life, very much less of this parochial spirit
than there was formerly. Still there is
an occasional outcropping here and there;
and it is just as well that we should keep
steadily in mind the futility of talking of
a Northern literature or a Southern literature, an Eastern or a Western school of
art or science. Joel Chandler Harris is

emphatically a national writer; so is Mark
Twain. They do not write merely for
Georgia or Missouri or California any
more than for Illinois or Connecticut;
they write as Americans and for all people who can read English. St. Gaudens
lives in New York; but his work is just
as distinctive of Boston or Chicago. It
is of very great consequence that we
should have a full and ripe literary development in the United States, but it is
not of the least consequence whether New
York, or Boston, or Chicago, or San
Francisco becomes the literary or artistic
centre of the United States.

There is a second side to this question
of a broad Americanism, however. The
patriotism of the village or the belfry is
bad, but the lack of all patriotism is even
worse. There are philosophers who as-
sure us that in the future patriotism will
be regarded not as a virtue at all, but
merely as a mental stage in the jour-
ney toward a state of feeling when our

patriotism will include the whole human race and all the world. This may be so; but the age of which these philosophers speak is still several æons distant. In fact, philosophers of this type are so very advanced that they are of no practical service to the present generation. It may be that in ages so remote that we cannot now understand any of the feelings of those who will dwell in them, patriotism will no longer be regarded as a virtue, exactly as it may be that in those remote ages people will look down upon and disregard monogamic marriage; but as things now are and have been for two or three thousand years past, and are likely to be for two or three thousand years to come, the words "home" and "country" mean a great deal. Nor do they show any tendency to lose their significance. At present, treason, like adultery, ranks as one of the worst of all possible crimes.

One may fall very far short of treason and yet be an undesirable citizen in the community. The man who becomes Europeanized, who loses his power of doing good work on this side of the water, and who loses his love for his native land, is not a traitor; but he is a silly and undesirable citizen. He is as emphatically a noxious element in our body politic as is the man who comes here from abroad and remains a foreigner. Nothing will more quickly or more surely disqualify a man from doing good work in the world than the acquirement of that flaccid habit of mind which its possessors style cosmopolitanism.

It is not only necessary to Americanize the immigrants of foreign birth who settle among us, but it is even more necessary for those among us who are by birth and descent already Americans not to throw away our birthright, and, with incredible and contemptible folly, wander back to bow down before the alien gods whom our forefathers forsook. It is hard to believe that there is any necessity to warn

37

Americans that, when they seek to model themselves on the lines of other civilizations, they make themselves the butts of all right-thinking men; and yet the necessity certainly exists to give this warning to many of our citizens who pride themselves on their standing in the world of art and letters, or, perchance, on what they would style their social leadership in the community. It is always better to be an original than an imitation, even when the imitation is of something better than the original; but what shall we say of the fool who is content to be an imitation of something worse? Even if the weaklings who seek to be other than Americans were right in deeming other nations to be better than their own, the fact yet remains that to be a first-class American is fifty-fold better than to be a second-class imitation of a Frenchman or Englishman. As a matter of fact, however, those of our countrymen who do believe in American inferiority are always individuals who, however cultivated, have some organic weakness in their moral or mental make-up ; and the great mass of our people, who are robustly patriotic, and who have sound, healthy minds, are justified in regarding these feeble renegades with a half-impatient and half-amused scorn.

We believe in waging relentless war on rank-growing evils of all kinds, and it makes no difference to us if they happen to be of purely native growth. We grasp at any good, no matter whence it comes. We do not accept the evil attendant upon another system of government as an adequate excuse for that attendant upon our own; the fact that the courtier is a scamp does not render the demagogue any the less a scoundrel. But it remains true that, in spite of all our faults and shortcomings, no other land offers such glorious possibilities to the man able to take advantage of them as does ours; it remains true that no one of our people can do any work really worth doing unless he does it primarily as an American. It is because certain classes of our people still retain their spirit of colonial dependence on, and exaggerated deference to, European opinion, that they fail to accomplish what they ought to. It is precisely along the lines where we have worked most independently that we have accomplished the greatest results; and it is in those professions where there has been no servility to, but merely a wise profiting by, foreign experience, that we have produced our greatest men. Our soldiers and statesmen and orators; our explorers, our wilderness-winners and commonwealth-builders; the men who have made our laws and seen that they were executed; and the other men whose energy and ingenuity have created our marvellous material prosperity,—all these have been men who have drawn wisdom from the experience of every age and nation, but who have nevertheless thought, and worked, and conquered, and lived, and died purely as Americans; and on the whole they have done better work than has been done in any other country during the short period of our national life.

On the other hand, it is in those professions where our people have striven hardest to mould themselves in conventional European forms that they have succeeded least; and this holds true to the present day, the failure being of course most conspicuous where the man takes up his abode in Europe; where he becomes a second-rate European, because he is over-civilized, over-sensitive, over-refined, and has lost the hardihood and manly courage by which alone he can conquer in the keen struggle of our national life. Be it remembered, too, that this same being does not really become a European; he only ceases being an American, and becomes nothing. He throws away a great prize for the sake of a lesser one, and does not even get the lesser one. The

painter who goes to Paris, not merely to
get two or three years' thorough training in his art, but with the deliberate
purpose of taking up his abode there, and
with the intention of following in the ruts
worn deep by ten thousand earlier travel-
lers, instead of striking off to rise or fall
on a new line, thereby forfeits all chance
of doing the best work. He must content himself with aiming at that kind
of mediocrity which consists in doing
fairly well what has already been done
better; and he usually never even sees the
grandeur and picturesqueness lying open
before the eyes of every man who can
read the book of America's past and the
book of America's present. Thus it is
with the undersized man of letters, who
flees his country because he, with his
delicate, effeminate sensitiveness, finds
the conditions of life on this side of the
water crude and raw; in other words, because he finds that he cannot play a
man's part among men, and so goes where

he will be sheltered from the winds that harden stouter souls. This *émigré* may write graceful and pretty verses, essays, novels; but he will never do work to compare with that of his brother who is strong enough to stand on his own feet and do his work as an American. Thus it is with the scientist who spends his youth in a German university, and can thenceforth work only in the fields already fifty times furrowed by the German ploughs. Thus it is with that most foolish of parents who sends his children to be educated abroad, not knowing—what every clear-sighted man from Washington and Jay down has known—that the American who is to make his way in America should be brought up among his fellow Americans. It is among the people who like to consider themselves, and, indeed, to a large extent, are the leaders of the so-called social world, especially in some of the northeastern cities, that this colonial habit of thought, this thoroughly provincial spirit of admiration for things foreign and inability to stand on one's own feet, becomes most evident and most despicable. We believe in every kind of honest and lawful pleasure, so long as the getting it is not made man's chief business; and we believe heartily in the good that can be done by men of leisure who work hard in their leisure, whether at politics or philanthropy, literature or art. But a leisure class whose leisure simply means idleness is a curse to the community, and in so far as its members distinguish themselves chiefly by aping the worst—not the best—traits of similar people across the water, they become both comic and noxious elements of the body politic.

The third sense in which the word "Americanism" may be employed is with reference to the Americanizing of the newcomers to our shores. We must Americanize them in every way, in speech, in political ideas and principles, and in their way of looking at the relations between Church and State. We welcome the German or the Irishman who becomes an American. We have no use for the German or Irishman who remains such. We do not wish German-Americans and Irish-Americans who figure as such in our social and political life ; we want only Americans, and, provided they are such, we do not care whether they are of native or of Irish or of German ancestry. We have no room in any healthy American community for a German-American vote or an Irish-American vote, and it is contemptible demagogy to put planks into any party platform with the purpose of catching such a vote. We have no room for any people who do not act and vote simply as Americans, and as nothing else. Moreover, we have as little use for people who carry religious prejudices into our politics as for those who carry prejudices of caste or nationality. We stand unalterably in favor of the public-school system in its entirety. We believe that English and no other language is that in which all the school exercises should be conducted. We are against any division of the school fund, and against any appropriation of public money for sectarian purposes. We are against any recognition whatever by the State in any shape or form of State-aided parochial schools. But we are equally opposed to any discrimination against or for a man because of his creed. We demand that all citizens, Protestant and Catholic, Jew and Gentile, shall have fair treatment in every way; that all alike shall have their rights guaranteed them. The very reasons that make us unqualified in our opposition to State-aided sectarian schools make us equally bent that, in the management of our public schools, the adherents of each creed shall be given exact and equal justice, wholly without regard to their religious affiliations; that trustees, superintendents, teachers, scholars, all alike, shall be treated without any reference whatsoever to the creed they profess. We maintain that it is an outrage, in voting for a man for any position, whether State or national, to take into account his religious faith, provided only he is a good American. When a secret society does what in some places the American Protective Association seems to have done, and tries to proscribe Catholics both politically and socially, the members of such society show that they themselves are as utterly un-American, as alien to our school of political thought, as the worst immigrants who land on our shores. Their conduct is equally base and contemptible; they are the worst foes of our public-school system, because they strengthen the hands of its ultramontane enemies; they should receive the hearty condemnation of all Americans who are truly patriotic.

The mighty tide of immigration to our shores has brought in its train much of good and much of evil; and whether the good or the evil shall predominate depends mainly on whether these newcomers do or do not throw themselves heartily into our national life, cease to be European, and become Americans like the rest of us. More than a third of the people of the Northern States are of foreign birth or parentage. An immense number of them have become completely Americanized, and these stand on exactly the same plane as the descendants of any Puritan, Cavalier, or Knickerbocker among us, and do their full and honorable share of the nation's work. But where immigrants or the sons of immigrants, do not heartily and in good faith throw in their lot with us, but cling to the speech, the customs, the ways of life, and the habits of thought of the Old World which they have left, they thereby harm both themselves and us. If they remain alien elements, unassimilated, and with interests separate from ours, they are mere obstructions to the current of our national life, and, moreover, can get no good from it themselves. In fact, though we ourselves also suffer from their perversity, it is they who really suffer most. It is an immense benefit to the European immigrant to change him into an American citizen. To bear the name of American is to bear the most honorable of titles; and whoever does not so believe has no business to bear the name at all, and, if he comes from Europe, the sooner he goes back there the better. Besides, the man who does not become Americanized nevertheless fails to remain a European, and becomes nothing at all. The immigrant cannot possibly remain what he was, or continue to be a member of the Old-World society. If he tries to retain his old language, in a few generations it becomes a barbarous jargon; if he tries to retain his old customs and ways of life, in a few generations he becomes an uncouth boor. He has cut himself off from the Old World, and cannot retain his connection with it; and if he wishes

ever to amount to anything he must
throw himself heart and soul, and without reservation, into the new life to which
he has come. It is urgently necessary to
check and regulate our immigration by
much more drastic laws than now exist;
and this should be done both to keep out
laborers who tend to depress the labor
market, and to keep out races which do
not assimilate readily with our own, and
unworthy individuals of all races — not
only criminals, idiots, and paupers, but
anarchists of the Most and O'Donovan
Rossa type.

From his own standpoint, it is beyond
all question the wise thing for the immigrant to become thoroughly Americanized. Moreover, from our standpoint, we
have a right to demand it. We freely
extend the hand of welcome and of good-
fellowship to every man, no matter what
his creed or birthplace, who comes here
honestly intent on becoming a good
United States citizen like the rest of us;

but we have a right and it is our duty to demand that he shall indeed become so, and shall not confuse the issues with which we are struggling by introducing among us Old-World quarrels and prejudices. There are certain ideas which he must give up. For instance, he must learn that American life is incompatible with the existence of any form of anarchy, or of any secret society having murder for its aim, whether at home or abroad; and he must learn that we exact full religious toleration and the complete separation of Church and State. Moreover, he must not bring in his Old-World religious race and national antipathies, but must merge them into love for our common country, and must take pride in the things which we can all take pride in. He must revere only our flag; not only must it come first, but no other flag should even come second. He must learn to celebrate Washington's birthday rather than that of the Queen or Kaiser, and the Fourth of July instead of St. Patrick's Day. Our political and social questions must be settled on their own merits, and not complicated by quarrels between England and Ireland, or France and Germany, with which we have nothing to do; it is an outrage to fight an American political campaign with reference to questions of European politics. Above all, the immigrant must learn to talk and think and *be* United States.

The immigrant of to-day can learn much from the experience of the immigrants of the past, who came to America prior to the Revolutionary War. We were then already, what we are now, a people of mixed blood. Many of our most illustrious Revolutionary names were borne by men of Huguenot blood — Jay, Sevier, Marion, Laurens. But the Huguenots were, on the whole, the best immigrants we have ever received ; sooner than any other, and more completely, they became American in speech, conviction, and thought. The Hollanders took longer than the Huguenots to become completely assimilated ; nevertheless they in the end became so, immensely to their own advantage. One of the leading Revolutionary generals, Schuyler, and one of the Presidents of the United States, Van Buren, were of Dutch blood ; but they rose to their positions, the highest in the land, because they had become Americans and had ceased being Hollanders. If they had remained members of an alien body, cut off by their speech and customs and belief from the rest of the American community, Schuyler would have lived his life as a boorish, provincial squire, and Van Buren would have ended his days a small tavern-keeper. So it is with the Germans of Pennsylvania. Those of them who became Americanized have furnished to our history a multitude of honorable names, from the days of the Mühlenbergs onward ; but those who did not become

Americanized form to the present day an unimportant body, of no significance in American existence. So it is with the Irish, who gave to Revolutionary annals such names as Carroll and Sullivan, and to the Civil War men like Sheridan—men who were Americans and nothing else : while the Irish who remain such, and busy themselves solely with alien politics, can have only an unhealthy influence upon American life, and can never rise as do their compatriots who become straight-out Americans. Thus it has ever been with all people who have come hither, of whatever stock or blood. The same thing is true of the churches. A church which remains foreign, in language or spirit, is doomed.

But I wish to be distinctly understood on one point. Americanism is a question of spirit, conviction, and purpose, not of creed or birthplace. The politician who bids for the Irish or German vote, or the Irishman or German who votes as an

Irishman or German, is despicable, for all citizens of this commonwealth should vote solely as Americans ; but he is not a whit less despicable than the voter who votes against a good American, merely because that American happens to have been born in Ireland or Germany. Know-nothingism, in any form, is as utterly un-American as foreignism. It is a base outrage to oppose a man because of his religion or birthplace, and all good citizens will hold any such effort in abhorrence. A Scandinavian, a German, or an Irishman who has really become an American has the right to stand on exactly the same footing as any native-born citizen in the land, and is just as much entitled to the friendship and support, social and political, of his neighbors. Among the men with whom I have been thrown in close personal contact socially, and who have been among my staunchest friends and allies politically, are not a few Americans who happen to have been born on the other side of the water, in Germany, Ireland, Scandinavia; and there could be no better men in the ranks of our native-born citizens.

In closing, I cannot better express the ideal attitude that should be taken by our fellow-citizens of foreign birth than by quoting the words of a representative American, born in Germany, the Honorable Richard Guenther of Wisconsin. In a speech spoken at the time of the Samoan trouble, he said:

"We know as well as any other class of American citizens where our duties belong. We will work for our country in time of peace and fight for it in time of war, if a time of war should ever come. When I say our country, I mean, of course, our adopted country. I mean the United States of America. After passing through the crucible of naturalization, we are no longer Germans; we are Americans. Our attachment to America cannot be measured by the length of our residence here. We are Americans from the moment we touch the American shore until we are laid in American graves. We will fight for America whenever necessary. America, first, last, and all the time. America against Germany, America against the world; America, right or wrong; always America. We are Americans."

All honor to the man who spoke such words as those; and I believe they express the feelings of the great majority of those among our fellow-American citizens who were born abroad. We Americans can only do our allotted task well if we face it steadily and bravely, seeing but not fearing the dangers. Above all we must stand shoulder to shoulder, not asking as to the ancestry or creed of our comrades, but only demanding that they be in very truth Americans, and that we all work together, heart, hand, and head, for the honor and greatness of our common country.

MORALITY AND EFFICIENCY

SOMETIMES, in addressing men who
sincerely desire the betterment of
our public affairs, but who have not
taken active part in directing them, I
feel tempted to tell them that there are
two gospels which should be preached to
every reformer. The first is the gospel
of morality; the second is the gospel of
efficiency.

To decent, upright citizens it is hardly
necessary to preach the doctrine of morality as applied to the affairs of public life.
It is an even graver offence to sin against
the commonwealth than to sin against
an individual. The man who debauches
our public life, whether by malversation
of funds in office, by the actual bribery of

voters or of legislators, or by the corrupt use of the offices as spoils wherewith to reward the unworthy and the vicious for their noxious and interested activity in the baser walks of political life,—this man is a greater foe to our well-being as a nation than is even the defaulting cashier of a bank, or the betrayer of a private trust.   No amount of intelligence and no amount of energy will save a nation which is not honest, and no government can ever be a permanent success if administered in accordance with base ideals.   The first requisite in the citizen who wishes to share the work of our public life, whether he wishes himself to hold office or merely to do his plain duty as an American by taking part in the management of our political machinery, is that he shall act disinterestedly and with a sincere purpose to serve the whole commonwealth.

But disinterestedness and honesty and unselfish desire to do what is right are

not enough in themselves. A man must
not only be disinterested, but he must be
efficient. If he goes into politics he
must go into practical politics, in order
to make his influence felt. Practical politics must not be construed to mean dirty
politics. On the contrary, in the long
run the politics of fraud and treachery
and foulness are unpractical politics, and
the most practical of all politicians is the
politician who is clean and decent and
upright. But a man who goes into the
actual battles of the political world must
prepare himself much as he would for
the struggle in any other branch of our
life. He must be prepared to meet men
of far lower ideals than his own, and to
face things, not as he would wish them,
but as they are. He must not lose his own
high ideal, and yet he must face the fact
that the majority of the men with whom
he must work have lower ideals. He
must stand firmly for what he believes,
and yet he must realize that political

action, to be effective, must be the joint action of many men, and that he must sacrifice somewhat of his own opinions to those of his associates if he ever hopes to see his desires take practical shape.

The prime thing that every man who takes an interest in politics should remember is that he must act, and not merely criticise the actions of others. It is not the man who sits by his fireside reading his evening paper and saying how bad our politics and politicians are who will ever do anything to save us; it is the man who goes out into the rough hurly-burly of the caucus, the primary, and the political meeting, and there faces his fellows on equal terms. The real service is rendered, not by the critic who stands aloof from the contest, but by the man who enters into it and bears his part as a man should, undeterred by the blood and sweat. It is a pleasant but a dangerous thing to associate merely with cultivated, refined men of high ideals and sincere purpose to do right and to think that one has done all one's duty by discussing politics with such associates. It is a good thing to meet men of this stamp; indeed it is a necessary thing, for we thereby brighten our ideals and keep in touch with the people who are unselfish in their purposes; but if we associate with such men exclusively we can accomplish nothing. The actual battle must be fought out on other and less pleasant fields. The actual advance must be made in the field of practical politics among the men who represent or guide or control the mass of the voters, the men who are sometimes rough and coarse, who sometimes have lower ideals than they should, but who are capable, masterful, and efficient. It is only by mingling on equal terms with such men, by showing them that one is able to give and to receive heavy punishment without flinching, and that one can master the details of political management as well as

5

they can, that it is possible for a man to establish a standing that will be useful to him in fighting for a great reform. Every man who wishes well to his country is in honor bound to take an active part in political life. If he does his duty and takes that active part he will be sure occasionally to commit mistakes and to be guilty of shortcomings. For these mistakes and shortcomings he will receive the unmeasured denunciation of the critics who commit neither because they never do anything but criticise. Nevertheless he will have the satisfaction of knowing that the salvation of the country ultimately lies, not in the hands of his critics, but in the hands of those who, however imperfectly, actually do the work of the nation. I would not for one moment be understood as objecting to criticism or failing to appreciate its importance. We need fearless criticism of our public men and public parties; we need unsparing condemnation

of all persons and all principles that
count for evil in our public life; but it
behooves every man to remember that
the work of the critic, important though
it is, is of altogether secondary importance, and that, in the end, progress is
accomplished by the man who does the
things, and not by the man who talks
about how they ought or ought not to be
done.

Therefore the man who wishes to do
good in his community must go into active political life. If he is a Republican,
let him join his local Republican association; if a Democrat, the Democratic
association; if an Independent, then let
him put himself in touch with those who
think as he does. In any event let him
make himself an active force and make
his influence felt. Whether he works
within or without party lines he can
surely find plenty of men who are desirous of good government, and who,
if they act together, become at once a

67

power on the side of righteousness. Of course, in a government like ours, a man can accomplish anything only by acting in combination with others, and equally, of course, a number of people can act together only by each sacrificing certain of his beliefs or prejudices. That man is indeed unfortunate who cannot in any given district find some people with whom he can conscientiously act. He may find that he can do best by acting within a party organization; he may find that he can do best by acting, at least for certain purposes, or at certain times, outside of party organizations, in an independent body of some kind; but with some association he must act if he wishes to exert any real influence.

One thing to be always remembered is that neither independence on the one hand nor party fealty on the other can ever be accepted as an excuse for failure to do active work in politics. The party man who offers his allegiance to party as

an excuse for blindly following his party,
right or wrong, and who fails to try to
make that party in any way better, commits
a crime against the country; and a crime
quite as serious is committed by the independent who makes his independence an
excuse for easy self-indulgence, and who
thinks that when he says he belongs to
neither party he is excused from the duty
of taking part in the practical work of
party organizations. The party man is
bound to do his full share in party management. He is bound to attend the
caucuses and the primaries, to see that
only good men are put up, and to exert
his influence as strenuously against the
foes of good government within his party
as, through his party machinery, he does
against those who are without the party.
In the same way the independent, if he
cannot take part in the regular organizations, is bound to do just as much active
constructive work (not merely the work
of criticism) outside; he is bound to try

to get up an organization of his own and to try to make that organization felt in some effective manner. Whatever course the man who wishes to do his duty by his country takes in reference to parties or to independence of parties, he is bound to try to put himself in touch with men who think as he does, and to help make their joint influence felt in behalf of the powers that go for decency and good government. He must try to accomplish things; he must not vote in the air unless it is really necessary. Occasionally a man must cast a "conscience vote," when there is no possibility of carrying to victory his principles or his nominees; at times, indeed, this may be his highest duty; but ordinarily this is not the case. As a general rule a man ought to work and vote for something which there is at least a fair chance of putting into effect.

Yet another thing to be remembered by the man who wishes to make his influence felt for good in our politics is that he must act purely as an American. If he is not deeply imbued with the American spirit he cannot succeed. Any organization which tries to work along the line of caste or creed, which fails to treat all American citizens on their merits as men, will fail, and will deserve to fail. Where our political life is healthy, there is and can be no room for any movement organized to help or to antagonize men because they do or do not profess a certain religion, or because they were or were not born here or abroad. We have a right to ask that those with whom we associate, and those for whom we vote, shall be themselves good Americans in heart and spirit, unhampered by adherence to foreign ideals and acting without regard to the national and religious prejudices of European countries; but if they really are good Americans in spirit and thought and purpose, that is all that we have any right to consider in regard to them. In the

same way there must be no discrimination for or against any man because of
his social standing. On the one side,
there is nothing to be made out of a political organization which draws an ex-
clusive social line, and on the other it
must be remembered that it is just as un-
American to vote against a man because
he is rich as to vote against him because
he is poor. The one man has just as
much right as the other to claim to be
treated purely on his merits as a man.
In short, to do good work in politics, the
men who organize must organize wholly
without regard to whether their associates were born here or abroad, whether
they are Protestants or Catholics, Jews or
Gentiles, whether they are bankers or
butchers, professors or day-laborers. All
that can rightly be asked of one's political associates is that they shall be honest
men, good Americans, and substantially
in accord as regards their political ideas.

Another thing that must not be forgotten by the man desirous of doing good political work is the need of the rougher, manlier virtues, and above all the virtue of personal courage, physical as well as moral. If we wish to do good work for our country, we must be unselfish, disinterested, sincerely desirous of the well-being of the commonwealth, and capable of devoted adherence to a lofty ideal; but in addition we must be vigorous in mind and body, able to hold our own in rough conflict with our fellows, able to suffer punishment without flinching, and, at need, to repay it in kind with full interest. A peaceful and commercial civilization is always in danger of suffering the loss of the virile fighting qualities without which no nation, however cultured, however refined, however thrifty and prosperous, can ever amount to anything. Every citizen should be taught, both in public and in private life, that while he must avoid brawling and quarrelling, it is his duty to stand up for his rights. He must realize that the only man who is more contemptible than the blusterer and bully is the coward. No man is worth much to the commonwealth if he is not capable of feeling righteous wrath and just indignation, if he is not stirred to hot anger by misdoing, and is not impelled to see justice meted out to the wrong-doers. No man is worth much anywhere if he does not possess both moral and physical courage. A politician who really serves his country well, and deserves his country's gratitude, must usually possess some of the hardy virtues which we admire in the soldier who serves his country well in the field.

An ardent young reformer is very apt to try to begin by reforming too much. He needs always to keep in mind that he has got to serve as a sergeant before he assumes the duties of commander-in-chief. It is right for him from the beginning to take a great interest in National, State, and Municipal affairs, and to try to make himself felt in them if the occasion arises ; but the best work must be done by the citizen working in his own ward or district. Let him associate himself with the men who think as he does, and who, like him, are sincerely devoted to the public good. Then let them try to make themselves felt in the choice of alderman, of councilman, of assemblyman. The politicians will be prompt to recognize their power, and the people will recognize it, too, after a while. Let them organize and work, undaunted by any temporary defeat. If they fail at first, and if they fail again, let them merely make up their minds to redouble their efforts and perhaps alter their methods; but let them keep on working.

It is sheer unmanliness and cowardice to shrink from the contest because at first there is failure, or because the work is difficult or repulsive. No man who is worth his salt has any right to abandon the effort to better our politics merely because he does not find it pleasant, merely because it entails associations which to him happen to be disagreeable. Let him keep right on, taking the buffets he gets good-humoredly, and repaying them with heartiness when the chance arises. Let him make up his mind that he will have to face the violent opposition of the spoils politician, and also, too often, the unfair and ungenerous criticism of those who ought to know better. Let him be careful not to show himself so thin-skinned as to mind either ; let him fight his way forward, paying only so much regard to both as is necessary to enable him to win in spite of them. He may not, and indeed probably will not, accomplish nearly as much as he would like to, or as he thinks he ought to : but he will certainly accomplish something ; and if he can feel that he has helped to elevate the type of representative sent to the municipal, the State, or the national legislature from his district, or to elevate the standard of duty among the public officials in his own ward, he has a right to be profoundly satisfied with what he has accomplished.

Finally, there is one other matter which the man who tries to wake his fellows to higher political action would do well to ponder. It is a good thing to appeal to citizens to work for good government because it will better their estate materially, but it is a far better thing to appeal to them to work for good government because it is right in itself to do so. Doubtless, if we can have clean, honest politics, we shall be better off in material matters. A thoroughly pure, upright, and capable administration of the affairs of New York City results in a very appreciable increase of comfort to each citizen. We should have better systems of transportation ; we should have cleaner streets, better sewers, and the like. But it is sometimes difficult to show the individual citizen that he will be individually better

off in his business and in his home affairs
for taking part in politics. I do not think
it is always worth while to show that this
will always be the case. The citizen
should be appealed to primarily on the
ground that it is his plain duty, if he
wishes to deserve the name of freeman, to
do his full share in the hard and difficult
work of self-government. He must do
his share unless he is willing to prove
himself unfit for free institutions, fit only
to live under a government where he will
be plundered and bullied because he deserves to be plundered and bullied on
account of his selfish timidity and short-
sightedness. A clean and decent government is sure in the end to benefit our
citizens in the material circumstances of
their lives; but each citizen should be
appealed to to take part in bettering
our politics, not for the sake of any possible improvement it may bring to his affairs, but on the ground that it is his
plain duty to do so, and that this is a

duty which it is cowardly and dishonorable in him to shirk.

To sum up, then, the men who wish to work for decent politics must work practically, and yet must not swerve from their devotion to a high ideal. They must actually do things, and not merely confine themselves to criticising those who do them. They must work disinterestedly, and appeal to the disinterested element in others, although they must also do work which will result in the material betterment of the community. They must act as Americans through and through, in spirit and hope and purpose, and, while being disinterested, unselfish, and generous in their dealings with others, they must also show that they possess the essential manly virtues of energy, of resolution, and of indomitable personal courage.

NATIONAL LIFE AND CHARACTER

NATIONAL LIFE AND CHARACTER

IN *National Life and Character; a Forecast*, Mr. Charles H. Pearson, late fellow of Oriel College, Oxford, and sometime Minister of Education in Victoria, has produced one of the most notable books of the end of the century. Mr. Pearson is not always quite so careful as he might be about his facts; many of the conclusions he draws from them seem somewhat strained; and with much of his forecast most of us would radically disagree. Nevertheless, no one can read this book without feeling his thinking powers greatly stimulated; without being forced to ponder problems of which he was previously wholly ignorant, or which

he but half understood ; and without
realizing that he is dealing with the work
of a man of lofty thought and of deep and
philosophic insight into the world-forces
of the present.

Mr. Pearson belongs to the melancholy
or pessimist school, which has become so
prominent in England during the last
two or three decades, and which has been
represented there for half a century. In
fact, the note of despondency seems to be
the dominant note among Englishmen of
high cultivation at the present time. It
is as marked among their statesmen and
publicists as among their men of letters,
Mr. Balfour being particularly happy in
his capacity to express in good English,
and with much genuine elevation of
thought, a profound disbelief in nineteenth-century progress, and an equally
profound distrust of the future toward
which we are all travelling.

For much of this pessimism and for
many of the prophecies which it evokes

there is no excuse whatsoever. There
may possibly be good foundation for the
pessimism as to the future shown by men
like Mr. Pearson; but hitherto the writers
of the stamp of the late " Cassandra "
Greg who have been pessimistic about
the present, have merely betrayed their
own weakness or their own incapacity to
judge contemporary persons and events.
The weakling, the man who cannot struggle with his fellow-men and with the conditions that surround him, is very apt to
think these men and these conditions
bad; and if he has the gift of writing, he
puts these thoughts down at some length
on paper. Very strong men, moreover,
if of morose and dyspeptic temper, are
apt to rail at the present, and to praise
the past simply because they do not live
in it. To any man who will consider the
subject from a scientific point of view,
with a desire to get at the truth, it is
needless to insist on the fact that at no
period of the world's history has there

been so much happiness generally diffused among mankind as now.

At no period of the world's history has life been so full of interest and of possibilities of excitement and enjoyment as for us who live in the latter half of the nineteenth century. This is not only true as far as the working classes are concerned, but it is especially true as regards the men of means, and above all of those men of means who also possess brains and ambition. Never before in the world's history have there been such opportunities thrown open to men, in the way of building new commonwealths, exploring new countries, conquering kingdoms, and trying to adapt the governmental policy of old nations to new and strange conditions. The half-century which is now closing has held out to the people who have dwelt therein some of the great prizes of history. Abraham Lincoln and Prince Bismarck have taken their places among the world's worthies. Mighty masters of war have arisen in America, in Germany, in Russia; Lee and Grant, Jackson and Farragut, Moltke, Skobeleff, and the Red Prince. The work of the chiefs of mechanical and electrical invention has never been equalled before, save perhaps by what was done in the first half of this same century. Never before have there been so many opportunities for commonwealth builders; new States have been pitched on the banks of the Saskatchewan, the Columbia, the Missouri, and the Colorado, on the seacoast of Australia, and in the interior of Central Africa. Vast regions have been won by the sword. Burmah and Turkestan, Egypt and Matabeleland, have rewarded the prowess of English and Russian conquerors, exactly as, when the glory of Rome was at its height, remote Mediterranean provinces furnished triumphs to the great military leaders of the Eternal City. English administrators govern subject empires larger than those conquered by Alexander. In letters no name has been produced that will stand with the first half-dozen of all literature, but there have been very many borne by men whose effect upon the literatures of their own countries has been profound, and whose works will last as long as the works of any men written in the same tongues. In science even more has been done ; Darwin has fairly revolutionized thought ; and many others stand but a step below him.

All this means only that the opportunities have been exceptionally great for the men of exceptionally great powers ; but they have also been great for the men of ordinary powers. The workingman is, on the whole, better fed, better clothed, better housed, and provided with greater opportunities for pleasure and for mental and spiritual improvement than ever before. The man with ability enough to become a lawmaker has the fearful joy of grappling with problems as important as any the administrators and legislators of the past had to face. The ordinary man of adventurous tastes and a desire to get all out of life that can be gotten is beyond measure better off than were his forefathers of one, two, or three centuries back. He can travel round the world; he can dwell in any country he wishes; he can explore strange regions; he can spend years by himself in the wilderness, hunting great game; he can take part in a campaign here and there. Whithersoever his tastes lead him, he finds that he has far greater capacity conferred upon him by the conditions of nineteenth-century civilization to do something of note than ever a man of his kind had before. If he is observant, he notes all around him the play of vaster forces than have ever before been exerted, working, half blindly, half under control, to bring about immeasurable results. He sees going on before his eyes a great transfer of population and civilization,

which is making America north of the
Rio Grande and Australia English-
speaking continents ; which has filled
Central and South America with States
of uncertain possibilities; which is cre-
ating for the first time a huge Aryan
nation across the entire north of Asia,
and which is working changes in Africa
infinitely surpassing in importance all
those that have ever taken place there
since the days when the Bantu peoples
first built their beehive huts on the banks
of the Congo and the Zambezi. Our
century has teemed with life and interest.

Yet this is the very century at which
Carlyle railed; and it is strange to think
that he could speak of the men at that
very moment engaged in doing such
deeds, as belonging to a worn-out age.
His vision was clear to see the importance and the true bearing of England's
civil war of the seventeenth century, and
yet he remained mole-blind to the
vaster and more important civil war

waged before his very eyes in nineteenth-century America. The heroism
of Naseby and Worcester and Minden
hid from him the heroism of Balaklava
and Inkerman, of Lucknow and Delhi.
He could appreciate at their worth the
campaigns of the Seven Years' War,
and yet could hardly understand those
waged between the armies of the Poto-
mac and of Northern Virginia. He was
fairly inspired by the fury and agony
and terror of the struggle at Kunners-
dorf; and yet could not appreciate the
immensely greater importance of the
death-wrestle that reeled round Gettysburg. His eyes were so dazzled by the
great dramas of the past that he could
not see the even greater drama of the
present. It is but the bare truth to say
that never have the rewards been greater,
never has there been more chance for
doing work of great and lasting value,
than this last half of the nineteenth century has offered alike to statesman and

soldier, to explorer and commonwealth-builder, to the captain of industry, to the man of letters, and to the man of science. Never has life been more interesting to each to take part in. Never has there been a greater output of good work done both by the few and by the many.

Nevertheless, signs do not fail that we are on the eve of great changes, and that in the next century we shall see the conditions of our lives, national and individual, modified after a sweeping and radical fashion. Many of the forces that make for national greatness and for individual happiness in the nineteenth century will be absent entirely, or will act with greatly diminished strength, in the twentieth. Many of the forces that now make for evil will by that time have gained greatly in volume and power. It is foolish to look at the future with blind and careless optimism; quite as foolish as to gaze at it only through the dun-colored mists that surround the preachers of pessimism. It is always best to look at facts squarely in the face, without blinking them, and to remember that, as has been well said, in the long run even the most uncomfortable truth is a safer companion than the pleasantest falsehood.

Whether the future holds good or evil for us does not, it is true, alter our duty in the present. We must stand up valiantly in the fight for righteousness and wisdom as we see them, and must let the event turn out as it may. Nevertheless, even though there is little use in pondering over the future, most men of intelligence do ponder over it at times, and if we think of it at all, it is well to think clearly.

Mr. Pearson writes a forecast of what he believes probably will, or at least very possibly may happen in the development of national life and character during the era upon which we are now entering. He is a man who has had exceptional advantages for his work; he has studied deeply and travelled widely; he has been a diligent reader of books and a keen observer of men. To a careful training in one of the oldest of the world's universities he has added long experience as an executive officer in one of the world's youngest commonwealths. He writes with power and charm. His book is interesting in manner, and is still more interesting in matter, for he has thought deeply and faithfully over subjects of immense importance to the future of all the human race. He possesses a mind of marked originality. Moreover, he always faithfully tries to see facts as they actually are. He is, it seems to me, unduly pessimistic; but he is not pessimistic of set purpose, nor does he adopt pessimism as a cult. He tries hard, and often successfully, to make himself see and to make himself state forces that are working for good. We may or may not differ from him,

but it behooves us, if we do, to state
our positions guardedly; for we are dealing with a man who has displayed much
research in getting at his facts and much
honesty in arriving at his rather melancholy conclusions.

The introduction to Mr. Pearson's
book is as readable as the chapters that
follow, and may best be considered in
connection with the first of these chapters, which is entitled "The Unchange-
able Limits of the Higher Races." I
am almost tempted to call this the most
interesting of the six chapters of the
book, and yet one can hardly do so
when absorbed in reading any one of
the other five. Mr. Pearson sees what
ought to be evident to every one, but
apparently is not, that what he calls the
"higher races," that is, the races that
for the last twenty-five hundred years
(but, it must be remembered, only during
the last twenty-five hundred years) have
led the world, can prosper only under

conditions of soil and climate analogous to those obtaining in their old European homes. Speaking roughly, this means that they can prosper only in the temperate zones, north and south.

Four hundred years ago the temperate zones were very thinly peopled indeed, while the tropical and sub-tropical regions were already densely populated. The great feature in the world's history for the last four centuries has been the peopling of these vast, scantily inhabited regions by men of the European stocks; notably by men speaking English, but also by men speaking Russian and Spanish. During the same centuries these European peoples have for the first time acquired an enormous ascendency over all other races. Once before, during the days of the Greco-Macedonian and Roman supremacy, European peoples possessed a somewhat similar supremacy; but it was not nearly as great, for at that period America and Australia were un-

known, Africa south of the Sahara was
absolutely unaffected by either Roman or
Greek, and all but an insignificant portion of Asia was not only without the
pale of European influence, but held
within itself immense powers of menace
to Europe, and contained old and peculiar civilizations, still flourishing in their
prime. All this has now been changed.
Great English-speaking nations have
sprung up in America north of the Rio
Grande, and are springing up in Australia.
The Russians, by a movement which has
not yet fired the popular imagination,
but which all thinking men recognize
as of incalculable importance, are building a vast State in Northern Asia,
stretching from the Yellow Sea to the
Ural Mountains. Tropical America is
parcelled out among States partly of
European blood, and mainly European
in thought, speech, and religion; while
tropical Asia and Africa have been
divided among European powers, and

7

are held in more or less complete sub-
jection by their military and civil agents.
It is no wonder that men who are content to look at things superficially, and
who think that the tendencies that have
triumphed during the last two centuries
are as immutable in their workings as
great natural laws, should speak as if it
were a mere question of time when the
civilized peoples should overrun and
occupy the entire world, exactly as they
now do Europe and North America.

Mr. Pearson points out with great clearness the groundlessness of this belief. He
deserves especial praise for discriminating
between the importance of ethnic and
of merely political conquests. The conquest by one country of another populous
country always attracts great attention at
the time, and has wide momentary effects;
but it is of insignificant importance when
compared with the kind of armed settlement which causes new nations of an old
stock to spring up in new countries. The

campaigns carried on by the lieutenants
of Justinian against Goth and Vandal,
Bulgarian and Persian seemed in the
eyes of civilized Europe at that time of
incalculably greater moment than the
squalid warfare being waged in England
between the descendants of Low Dutch
sea-thieves and the aboriginal British.
Yet, in reality, it was of hardly any consequence in history whether Belisarius
did or did not succeed in overthrowing
the Ostrogoth merely to make room for
the Lombard, or whether the Vandal did
or did not succumb to the Roman instead
of succumbing to the Saracen a couple
of centuries later; while it was of the
most vital consequence to the whole future of the world that the English should
supplant the Welsh as masters of Britain.

Again, in our own day, the histories
written of Great Britain during the last
century teem with her dealings with India,
while Australia plays a very insignificant
part indeed; yet, from the standpoint of

the ages, peopling of the great island-
continent with men of the English stock
is a thousand-fold more important than
the holding Hindoostan for a few centuries.

Mr. Pearson understands and brings
out clearly that in the long run a conquest must fail when it means merely the
erection of an insignificant governing
caste. He shows clearly that the men
of our stock do not prosper in tropical
countries. In the New World they leave
a thin strain of their blood among and
impose their laws, language, and forms
of government on the aboriginal races,
which then develop on new and dimly
drawn lines. In the Old World they fail
to do even this. In Asia they may leave
a few tens of thousands or possibly hundreds of thousands of Eurasians to form
an additional caste in a caste-ridden community. In tropical Africa they may
leave here and there a mulatto tribe like
the Griquas. But it certainly has not yet

been proved that the European can live and propagate permanently in the hot regions of India and Africa, and Mr. Pearson is right in anticipating for the whites who have conquered these tropical and sub-tropical regions of the Old World the same fate which befell the Greek kingdoms in Bactria and the Chersonese. The Greek rulers of Bactria were ultimately absorbed and vanished, as probably the English rulers of India will some day in the future—for the good of mankind, we sincerely hope and believe the very remote future—themselves be absorbed and vanish. In Africa south of the Zambezi (and possibly here and there on high plateaus north of it) there may remain white States, although even these States will surely contain a large colored population, always threatening to swamp the whites; but in tropical Africa generally it does not seem possible that any white State can ever be built up. Doubtless for many centuries European adventurers

and Arab raiders will rule over huge ter-
ritories in the country south of the Soudan and north of the Tropic of Capricorn,
and the whole structure, not only social,
but physical, of the negro and the negroid
peoples will be profoundly changed by
their influence and by the influence of the
half-caste descendants of these European
and Asiatic soldiers of fortune and industry. But it is hardly possible to conceive
that the peoples of Africa, however ultimately changed, will be anything but negroid in type of body and mind. It is
probable that the change will be in the
direction of turning them into tribes like
those of the Soudan, with a similar religion and morality. It is almost impossible that they will not in the end succeed
in throwing off the yoke of the European
outsiders, though this end may be, and
we hope will be, many centuries distant.
In America most of the West Indies are
becoming negro islands. The Spaniard,
however, because of the ease with which

he drops to a lower ethnic level, exerts a
much more permanent influence than
the Englishman upon tropic aboriginal
races ; and the tropical lands which the
Spaniards and Portuguese once held now
contain, and always will contain, races
which, though different from the Aryan
of the Temperate zone, yet bridge the
gulf between him and the black, red, and
yellow peoples who have dwelt from time
immemorial on both sides of the equator.

Taking all this into consideration, therefore, it is most likely that a portion of
Mr. Pearson's forecast, as regards the
people of the tropic zones, will be justified by events. It is impossible for the
dominant races of the temperate zones
ever bodily to displace the peoples of the
tropics. It is highly probable that these
people will cast off the yoke of their European conquerors sooner or later, and will
become independent nations once more;
though it is also possible that the modern
conditions of easy travel may permit the

permanent rule in the tropics of a vigorous northern race, renewed by a complete change every generation.

Mr. Pearson's further proposition is that these black, red, and yellow nations, when thus freed, will threaten the dominance of the higher peoples, possibly by military, certainly by industrial, rivalry, and that the mere knowledge of the equality of these stocks will cow and dispirit the higher races.

This part of his argument is open to very serious objections. In the first place, Mr. Pearson entirely fails to take into account the difference in character among the nationalities produced in the tropics as the result of European conquest. In Asia, doubtless, the old races now submerged by European predominance will reappear, profoundly changed in themselves and in their relations to one another, but as un-European as ever, and not appreciably affected by any intermixture of European blood. In Africa, the

native States will probably range somewhere between the Portuguese half-caste
and quarter-caste communities now existing on certain of the tropic coasts and
pastoral or agricultural communities, with
a Mohammedan religious cult and Asiatic
type of government, produced by the in-
fusion of a conquering semitic or hamitic
caste on a conquered negro people. There
may be a dominant caste of European
blood in some of these States, but that is
all. In tropical America, the change has
already taken place. The States that
there exist will not materially alter their
form. It is possible that here and there
populations of Chinese, pure or half-caste,
or even of coolies, may spring up ; but
taken as a whole, these States will be in
the future what they are now, that is,
they will be by blood partly white, but
chiefly Indian or negro, with their language, law, religion, literature, and governmental system approaching those of
Europe and North America.

Suppose that what Mr. Pearson foresees comes to pass, and that the black and yellow races of the world attain the same independence already achieved by the mongrel reddish race. Mr. Pearson thinks that this will expose us to two dangers. The first is that of actual physical distress caused by the competition of the teeming myriads of the tropics, or perhaps by their invasion of the Temperate zones. Mr. Pearson himself does not feel any very great anxiety about this invasion assuming a military type, and I think that even the fear he does express is unwarranted by the facts. He is immensely impressed by the teeming population of China. He thinks that the Chinese will some day constitute the dominant portion of the population, both politically and numerically, in the East Indies, New Guinea, and Farther India. In this he is probably quite right; but such a change would merely mean the destruction or submersion of Malay, Dyak, and Papuan

and would be of hardly any real consequence to the white man. He further
thinks that the Chinese may jeopardize
Russia in Asia. Here I am inclined to
think he is wrong. As far as it is possible to judge in the absence of statistics,
the Chinaman at present is not increasing
relatively as fast as the Slav and the
Anglo-Saxon. Half a century or so more
will put both of them within measurable
distance of equality with him, even in
point of numbers. The movement of
population in China is toward the south,
not the north; the menace is real for the
English and French protectorates in the
south; in the north the difficulty hitherto
has been to keep Russian settlers from
crossing the Chinese frontier. When the
great Trans - Siberian railroad is built,
and when a few millions more of Russian
settlers stretch from the Volga to the
valley of the Amoor, the danger of a
military advance by the Chinese against
Asiatic Russia will be entirely over, even

granting that it now exists. The Chinaman never has been, and probably never
will be, such a fighter as Turk or Tartar,
and he would have to possess an absolutely
overwhelming superiority of numbers to
give him a chance in a war of aggression
against a powerful military race. As yet,
he has made no advance whatever towards
developing an army capable of offensive
work against European foes. In China
there are no roads; the military profes-
sion is looked down on; Chinese troops
would be formidable only under a European leader, and a European leader would
be employed only from dire necessity;
that is to repel, not to undertake an invasion. Moreover, China is merely an aggregate of provinces with a central knot
at Pekin; and Pekin could be taken at
any time by a small trained army. China
will not menace Siberia until after under-
going some stupendous and undreamed-
of internal revolution. It is scarcely
within the bounds of possibility to con-

ceive of the Chinaman expelling the
European settler from lands in which
that settler represents the bulk of a fairly
thick population, not merely a small in-
trusive caste. It is, of course, always
possible that in the far-distant future
(though there is no sign of it now) China
may travel on the path of Japan, may
change her policy, may develop fleets and
armies; but if she does do this, there is
no reason why this fact should stunt and
dwarf the people of the higher races. In
Elizabeth's day the Turkish fleets and
armies stood towards those of European
powers in a far higher position than those
of China, or of the tropics generally, can
ever hope to stand in relation to the peoples of the Temperate zones; and yet this
did not hinder the Elizabethan Age from
being one of great note both in the field
of thought and in the field of action.

The anticipation of what might happen
if India became solidified seems even
more ill-founded. Here Mr. Pearson's

position is that the very continuance of
European rule, doing away with war and
famine, produces an increase of population and a solidity of the country, which
will enable the people to overthrow that
European rule. He assumes that the solidified and populous country will continue to remain such after the overthrow
of the Europeans, and will be capable of
deeds of aggression; but, of course, such
an assumption is contrary to all probabilities. Once the European rule was re-
moved, famine and internecine war would
again become chronic, and India would
sink back to her former place. Moreover,
the long continuance of British rule undoubtedly weakens the warlike fibre of
the natives, and makes the usurer rather
than the soldier the dominant type.

The danger to which Mr. Pearson al-
ludes, that even the negro peoples may in
time become vast military powers, con-
stituting a menace to Europe, really
seems to belong to a period so remote

that every condition will have changed to a degree rendering it impossible for us to make any estimate in reference thereto. By that time the descendant of the negro may be as intellectual as the Athenian. Even prophecy must not look too many thousand years ahead. It is perfectly possible that European settlements in Africa will be swamped some time by the rising of natives who outnumber them a hundred or a thousand to one, but it is not possible that the negroes will form a military menace to the people of the north, at least for a space of time longer than that which now separates us from the men of the River Drift. The negroid peoples, the so-called "hamitic," and bastard semitic, races of eastern middle Africa are formidable fighters; but their strength is not fit for any such herculean tasks.

There is much more reason to fear the industrial competition of these races; but even this will be less formidable as the powerof the State increases, and especially as the democratic idea obtains more and more currency. The Russians are not democratic at all, but the State is very powerful with them; and therefore they keep the Chinese out of their Siberian provinces, which are being rapidly filled up with a population mainly Slav, the remainder of which is being Slavicized. From the United States and Australia the Chinaman is kept out because the democracy, with much clearness of vision, has seen that his presence is ruinous to the white race.

Nineteenth-century democracy needs no more complete vindication for its existence than the fact that it has kept for the white race the best portions of the new worlds' surface, temperate America and Australia. Had these regions been under aristocratic governments, Chinese immigration would have been encouraged precisely as the slave trade is encouraged of necessity by any slave-holding oligarchy, and the result would in a few generations have been even more fatal to the white race; but the democracy, with the clear instinct of race selfishness, saw the race foe, and kept out the dangerous alien. The presence of the negro in our Southern States is a legacy from the time when we were ruled by a trans-oceanic aristocracy. The whole civilization of the future owes a debt of gratitude greater than can be expressed in words to that democratic policy which has kept the temperate zones of the new and the newest worlds a heritage for the white people.

As for the industrial competition, the Chinaman and the Hindoo may drive certain kinds of white traders from the tropics; but more than this they cannot do. They can never change the status of the white laborer in his own home, for the latter can always protect himself, and as soon as he is seriously menaced, always will protect himself, by protective tariffs and stringent immigration laws.

8

Mr. Pearson fears that when once the tropic races are independent, the white people will be humiliated and will lose heart; but this does not seem inevitable, and indeed seems very improbable. If the Englishman should lose his control over South Africa and India, it might indeed be a serious blow to the Englishman of Britain; though it may be well to remember that the generation of Englishmen which grew up immediately after England had lost America accomplished feats in arms, letters, and science such as, on the whole, no other English generation ever accomplished. Even granting that Britain were to suffer as Mr. Pearson thinks she would, the enormous majority of the English-speaking peoples, those whose homes are in America and Australia, would be absolutely unaffected; and Continental Europe would be little more affected than it was when the Portuguese and Dutch successively saw their African and Indian empires

diminish.   France has not been affected by the expulsion of the French from
Hayti; nor have the freed negroes of
Hayti been capable of the smallest ag-
gressive movement.   No American or
Australian cares in the least that the
tan-colored peoples of Brazil and Ecuador
now live under governments of their own
instead of being ruled by viceroys from
Portugal and Spain; and it is difficult
to see why they should be materially
affected by a similar change happening
in regard to the people along the Ganges
or the upper Nile.   Even if China does
become a military power on the European
model, this fact will hardly affect the
American and Australian at the end of
the twentieth century more than Japan's
effort to get admitted to the circle of
civilized nations has affected us at the
end of the nineteenth.

Finally, it must be borne in mind that if
any one of the tropical races ever does
reach a pitch of industrial and military

prosperity which makes it a menace to European and American countries, it will almost necessarily mean that this nation has itself become civilized in the process; and we shall then simply be dealing with another civilized nation of non-aryan blood, precisely as we now deal with Magyar, Fin, and Basque, without any thought of their being ethnically distinct from Croat, Rouman, or Wend.

In Mr. Pearson's second chapter he deals with the stationary order of society, and strives to show that while we are all tending toward it, some nations, notably France, have practically come to it. He adds that when this stationary stage is reached, it will produce general discouragement, and will probably affect the intellectual energy of the people concerned. He further points out that our races now tend to change from faith in private enterprises to faith in State organizations, and that this is likely to diminish the vigorous originality of any race. He even holds that we already see the beginning of a decadence, in the decline of speculative thought, and still more in the way of mechanical inventions. It is perfectly true that the *laissez-faire* doctrine of the old school of political economists is receiving less and less favor; but after all, if we look at events historically, we see that every race, as it has grown to civilized greatness, has used the power of the State more and more. A great State cannot rely on mere unrestricted individualism, any more than it can afford to crush out all individualism. Within limits, the mercilessness of private commercial warfare must be curbed as we have curbed the individual's right of private war power. It was not until the power of the State had become great in England, and until the lawless individualism of feudal times had vanished, that the English people began that career of greatness which has put them on a level with the

Greeks in point of intellectual achievement, and with the Romans in point of that material success which is measured by extension through settlement, by conquest, by triumphant warcraft and statecraft. As for Mr. Pearson's belief that we now see a decline in speculative thought and in mechanical invention, all that can be said is that the facts do not bear him out.

There is one side to this stationary state theory which Mr. Pearson scarcely seems to touch. He points out with emphasis the fact, which most people are prone to deny, that the higher orders of every society tend to die out; that there is a tendency, on the whole, for both lower classes and lower civilizations to increase faster than the higher. Taken in the rough, his position on this point is undoubtedly correct. Progressive societies, and the most progressive portions of society, fail to increase as fast as the others, and often positively decrease. The

great commanders, great statesmen, great
poets, great men of science of any period
taken together do not average as many
children who reach years of maturity as a
similar number of mechanics, workmen,
and farmers, taken at random. Nevertheless, society progresses, the improvement being due mainly to the transmission
of acquired characters, a process which in
every civilized State operates so strongly
as to counterbalance the operation of that
baleful law of natural selection which
tells against the survival of some of the
most desirable classes. Mr. Balfour, by
the way, whose forecast for the race is in
some respects not unlike Mr. Pearson's,
seems inclined to adopt the view that
acquired characteristics cannot be in-
herited; a position which, even though
supported by a few eminent names, is
hardly worthy serious refutation.

The point I wish to dwell upon here,
however, is that it is precisely in those
castes which have reached the stationary

state, or which are positively diminishing in numbers, that the highest culture and best training, the keenest enjoyment of life, and the greatest power of doing good to the community are to be found at present. Unquestionably no community that is actually diminishing in numbers is in a healthy condition: and as the world is now, with huge waste places still to fill up, and with much of the competition between the races reducing itself to the warfare of the cradle, no race has any chance to win a great place unless it consists of good breeders as well as of good fighters. But it may well be that these conditions will change in the future, when the other changes to which Mr. Pearson looks forward with such melancholy are themselves brought about. A nation sufficiently populous to be able to hold its own against aggression from without, a nation which, while developing the virtues of refinement, culture, and learning, has yet not lost those of courage, bold initiative, and military hardihood, might well play a great part in the world, even though it had come to that stationary state already reached by the dominant castes of thinkers and doers in most of the dominant races.

In Mr. Pearson's third chapter he dwells on some of the dangers of political development, and in especial upon the increase of the town at the expense of the country, and upon the growth of great standing armies. Excessive urban development undoubtedly does constitute a real and great danger. All that can be said about it is that it is quite impossible to prophesy how long this growth will continue. Moreover, some of the evils, as far as they really exist, will cure themselves. If townspeople do, generation by generation, tend to become stunted and weak, then they will die out, and the problem they cause will not be permanent ; while on the other hand, if the cities can be made healthy, both physically and morally, the objections to them must largely disappear. As for standing armies, Mr. Pearson here seems to have too much thought of Europe only. In America and Australia there is no danger of the upgrowing of great standing armies : and, as he well shows, the fact that every citizen must undergo military training is by no means altogether a curse to the nations of Continental Europe.

There is one point, by the way, although a small point, where it may be worth while to correct Mr. Pearson's statement of a fact. In dwelling on what is undoubtedly the truth, that raw militia are utterly incompetent to make head against trained regular forces, he finds it necessary to explain away the defeat at New Orleans. In doing this, he repeats the story as it has been told by British historians from Sir Archibald Alison to Goldwin Smith. I hasten to say that the misstatement is entirely natural on

Mr. Pearson's part; he was simply copying, without sufficiently careful investigation, the legend adopted by one side to take the sting out of defeat. The way he puts it is that six thousand British under Pakenham, without artillery, were hurled against strong works defended by twice their numbers, and were beaten, as they would have been beaten had the works been defended by almost any troops in the world. In the first place, Pakenham did not have six thousand men; he had almost ten thousand. In the second place, the Americans, instead of being twice as numerous as the British, were but little more than half as numerous. In the third place, so far from being without artillery, the British were much superior to the Americans in this respect. Finally, they assailed a position very much less strong than that held by Soult when Wellington beat him at Toulouse with the same troops which were defeated by Jackson at New Orleans. The simple truth is that Jackson was a very good general, and that he had under him troops whom he had trained in successive campaigns against Indians and Spaniards, and that on the three occasions when he brought Pakenham to battle — that is, the night attack, the great artillery duel, and the open assault — the English soldiers, though they fought with the utmost gallantry, were fairly and decisively beaten.

This one badly chosen premise does not, however, upset Mr. Pearson's conclusions. Plenty of instances can be taken from our war of 1812 to show how unable militia are to face trained regulars ; and an equally striking example was that afforded at Castlebar in Ireland, in 1798, when a few hundred French regulars attacked with the bayonet and drove in headlong flight from a very strong position, defended by a powerful artillery, five times their number of English, Scotch, and Irish militia.

In Mr. Pearson's fourth chapter he deals, from a very noble standpoint, with some advantages of national feeling. With this chapter and with his praise of patriotism, and particularly of that patriotism which attaches itself to the whole country, and not to any section of it, we can only express our hearty agreement.

In his fifth chapter, on "The Decline of the Family," he sets forth, or seems to set forth, certain propositions with which I must as heartily disagree. He seems to lament the change which is making the irresponsible despot as much of an anomaly in the family as in the State. He seems to think that this will weaken the family. It may do so, in some instances, exactly as the abolition of a despotism may produce anarchy ; but the movement is essentially as good in one case as in the other. To all who have known really happy family lives, that is to all who have known or have witnessed the greatest happiness which there can be on this earth, it is hardly necessary to say that the highest ideal of the family is attainable only where the father and mother stand to each other as lovers and friends, with equal rights. In these homes the children are bound to father and mother by ties of love, respect, and obedience which are simply strengthened by the fact that they are treated as reasonable beings with rights of their own, and that the rule of the household is changed to suit the changing years, as childhood passes into manhood and womanhood. In such a home the family is not weakened; it is strengthened. This is no unattainable ideal. Every one knows hundreds of homes where it is more or less perfectly realized, and it is an ideal incomparably higher than the ideal of the beneficent autocrat which it has so largely supplanted.

The final chapter of Mr. Pearson's book is entitled "The Decay of Character." He believes that our world is be-

coming a world with less adventure and
energy, less brightness and hope. He
believes that all the great books have
been written, all the great discoveries
made, all the great deeds done. He
thinks that the adoption of State socialism in some form will crush out individual merit and the higher kinds of
individual happiness. Of course, as to
this, all that can be said is that men
differ as to what will be the effect of the
forces whose working he portrays, and
that most of us who live in the American
democracy do not agree with him. It is
to the last degree improbable that State
socialism will ever be adopted in its ex-
treme form, save in a few places. It
exists, of course, to a certain extent
wherever a police force and a fire depart-
ment exist; and the sphere of the State's
action may be vastly increased without
in any way diminishing the happiness of
either the many or the few. It is even con-
ceivable that a combination of legislative

enactments and natural forces may greatly
reduce the inequalities of wealth without in any way diminishing the real
power of enjoyment or power for good
work of what are now the favored classes.
In our own country the best work has
always been produced by men who lived
in castes or social circles where the standard of essential comfort was high; that is,
where men were well clothed, well fed,
well housed, and had plenty of books
and the opportunity of using them; but
where there was small room for extrava-
gant luxury. We think that Mr. Pearson's fundamental error here is his belief
that the raising of the mass necessarily
means the lowering of the standard of life
for the fortunate few. Those of us who
now live in communities where the native
American element is largest and where
there is least inequality of conditions
know well that there is no reason whatever in the nature of things why, in the
future, communities should not spring up

where there shall be no great extremes
of poverty and wealth, and where, nevertheless, the power of civilization and the
chances for happiness and for doing good
work shall be greater than ever before.

As to what Mr. Pearson says about the
work of the world which is best worth
doing being now done, the facts do not
bear him out. He thinks that the great
poems have all been written, that the
days of the drama and the epic are past.
Yet one of the greatest plays that has
ever been produced, always excepting the
plays of Shakespeare, was produced in
this century; and if the world had to
wait nearly two thousand years after the
vanishing of the Athenian dramatists before Shakespeare appeared, and two hundred years more before Goethe wrote his
one great play, we can well afford to sus-
pend judgment for a few hundred years,
at least, before asserting that no country
and no language will again produce another great drama. So it is with the

9

epic. We are too near Milton, who came three thousand years after Homer, to assert that the centuries to come will never more see an epic. One race may grow feeble and decrepit and be unable to do any more work; but another may take its place. After a time the Greek and Latin writers found that they had no more to say; and a critic belonging to either nationality might have shaken his head and said that all the great themes had been used up and all the great ideas expressed; nevertheless, Dante, Cervantes, Molière, Schiller, Chaucer, and Scott, then all lay in the future.

Again, Mr. Pearson speaks of statecraft at the present day as offering fewer prizes and prizes of less worth than formerly, and as giving no chance for the development of men like Augustus Cæsar, Richelieu, or Chatham. It is difficult to perceive how these men can be considered to belong to a different class from Bismarck, who is yet alive; nor do we see

why any English-speaking people should
regard a statesman like Chatham, or far
greater than Chatham, as an impossi-
bility nowadays or in the future. We
Americans at least will with difficulty be
persuaded that there has ever been a time
when the nobler prize of achievement,
suffering, and success was offered to any
statesman than was offered both to Washington and to Lincoln. So, when Mr.
Pearson speaks of the warfare of civilized countries offering less chance to the
individual than the warfare of savage and
barbarous times, and of its being far less
possible now than in old days for a man
to make his personal influence felt in
warfare, we can only express our dis-
agreement. No world - conqueror can
arise save in or next to highly civilized
States. There never has been a barbarian
Alexander or Cæsar, Hannibal or Napo-
leon. Sitting Bull and Rain-in-the-Face
compare but ill with Von Moltke; and
no Norse king of all the heroic viking

age even so much as began to exercise
the influence upon the warfare of his
generation that Frederick the Great ex-
ercised on his.

It is not true that character of necessity
decays with the growth of civilization. It
may, of course, be true in some cases.
Civilization may tend to develop upon
the lines of Byzantine, Hindoo, and Inca;
and there are sections of Europe and
sections of the United States where we
now tend to pay heed exclusively to the
peaceful virtues and to develop only a
race of merchants, lawyers, and professors who will lack the virile qualities that
have made our race great and splendid.
This development may come, but it need
not come necessarily, and, on the whole,
the probabilities are against its coming
at all.

Mr. Pearson is essentially a man of
strength and courage. Looking into the
future the future seems to him gray and
unattractive; but he does not preach any

unmanly gospel of despair. He thinks that in time to come, though life will be freer than in the past from dangers and vicissitudes, yet it will contain fewer of the strong pleasures and of the opportunities for doing great deeds that are so dear to mighty souls. Nevertheless, he advises us all to front it bravely whether our hope be great or little; and he ends his book with these fine sentences: "Even so, there will still remain to us ourselves. Simply to do our work in life, and to abide the issue, if we stand erect before the eternal calm as cheerfully as our fathers faced the eternal unrest, may be nobler training for our souls than the faith in progress."

We do not agree with him that there will be only this eternal calm to face; we do not agree with him that the future holds for us a time when we shall ask nothing from the day but to live, nor from the future but that we may not deteriorate. We do not agree with him that there is a day approaching when the lower races will predominate in the world and the higher races will have lost their noblest elements. But after all it matters little what view we take of the future if, in our practice, we but do as he preaches, and face resolutely whatever fate may have in store. We ourselves are not certain that progress is assured; we only assert that it may be assured if we but live wise, brave, and upright lives. We do not know whether the future has in store for us calm or unrest. We cannot know beyond peradventure whether we can prevent the higher races from losing their nobler traits and from being overwhelmed by the lower races. On the whole, we think that the greatest victories are yet to be won, the greatest deeds yet to be done, and that there are yet in store for our peoples and for the causes that we uphold grander triumphs than have ever yet been scored. But be this as it may, we gladly agree that the

one plain duty of every man is to face the
future as he faces the present, regardless
of what it may have in store for him, and,
turning toward the light as he sees the
light, to play his part manfully, as a man
among men.